NOTES FROM THE UNDERGROUND

Borgo Press Books Translated by FRANK J. MORLOCK

Anna Karenina: A Play in Five Acts, by Edmond Guiraud, from the Novel by Leo Tolstoy
Anthony: A Play in Five Acts, by Alexandre Dumas, Père
The Children of Captain Grant: A Play in Five Acts, by Jules Verne and Adolphe d'Ennery
Crime and Punishment: A Play in Three Acts, by Frank J. Morlock, from the Novel by Fyodor Dostoyevsky
Don Quixote: A Play in Three Acts, by Victorien Sardou, from the Novel by Miguel de Cervantes Saavedra
Falstaff: A Play in Four Acts, by William Shakespeare, John Dennis, William Kendrick, and Frank J. Morlock
The Idiot: A Play in Three Acts, by Frank J. Morlock, from the Novel by Fyodor Dostoyevsky
Jesus of Nazareth: A Play in Three Acts, by Paul Demasy
Joan of Arc: A Play in Five Acts, by Charles Desnoyer
The Lily of the Valley: A Play in Five Acts, by Théodore Barrière and Arthur de Beauplan, from the Novel by Honoré de Balzac
The Man Who Saw the Devil: A Play in Two Acts, by Gaston Leroux
Michael Strogoff: A Play in Five Acts, by Adolphe d'Ennery and Jules Verne
The Mysteries of Paris: A Play in Five Acts, by Eugène Sue and Prosper Dinaux
Notes from the Underground: A Play in Two Acts, by Frank J. Morlock, from the Novel by Fyodor Dostoyevsky
Peau de Chagrin: A Play in Five Acts, by Louis Judicis, from the Novel by Honoré de Balzac
A Raw Youth: A Play in Five Acts, by Frank J. Morlock, from the Novel by Fyodor Dostoyevsky
Richard Darlington: A Play in Three Acts, by Alexandre Dumas, Père
The San Felice: A Play in Five Acts, by Maurice Drack, from the Novel by Alexander Dumas, Père
Shylock, the Merchant of Venice: A Play in Three Acts, by Alfred de Vigny
Socrates: A Play in Three Acts, by Voltaire
The Voyage Through the Impossible: A Play in Three Acts, by Adolphe d'Ennery and Jules Verne
William Shakespeare: A Play in Six Acts, by Ferdinand Dugué

NOTES FROM THE UNDERGROUND

A Play in Two Acts

by

Frank J. Morlock

Adapted from the Novel by Fyodor Dostoyevsky

The Borgo Press

An Imprint of Wildside Press LLC

MMIX

Copyright © 2009 by Frank J. Morlock

All rights reserved. No part of this book may be reproduced without the expressed written consent of the author. Professionals are warned that this material, being fully protected under the copyright laws of the United States of America, and all other countries of the Berne and Universal Copyright Convention, is subject to a royalty. All rights, including all forms of performance now existing or later invented, but not limited to professional, amateur, recording, motion picture, recitation, public reading, radio, television broadcasting, DVD, and Role Playing Games, and all rights of translation into foreign languages, are expressly reserved. Particular emphasis is placed on the question of readings, and all uses of these plays by educational institutions, permission for which must be secured in advance from the author's publisher, Wildside Press, 9710 Traville Gateway Dr. #234, Rockville, MD 20850 (phone 301-762-1305). Printed in the United States of America

www.wildsidebooks.com

FIRST WILDSIDE EDITION

CONTENTS

Cast of Characters 7

Act I, Scene 1 9
Act II, Scene 2 64
Act II, Scene 3 92

About the Author 95

DEDICATION

To My Friend and Doctor, Al Segal

CAST OF CHARACTERS

Man

Girl/Lisa

Apollon

Trudolyubov

Zerkov

ACT I.

Scene 1

The reception parlor of a Russian house of prostitution in the middle of the nineteenth century. The time is late at night. A cold wind blows outside. There is a noise of laughter offstage. Suddenly there is a violent knocking at the door. The lone girl in the room rouses herself and goes to the door.

Girl

Shh! Don't make so much noise.

(The knocking grows more insistent.)

Girl

Are you trying to ruin us? The police will come here.

(The girl opens the door and the Man rushes through the doorway.)

Man

Where are they, where are they?

Girl

What do you want? Are you sure you've got the right place?

Man

This is Madame Sophie's, isn't it?

Girl

Yes, but it's late. All the other girls have gone to bed.

Man

Look here, where are they?

Girl

Well, come in, will you? It's cold with the door open.

Man (coming in)

I beg you not to play games with me, I must find them.

Girl

Look, this is ridiculous—who is it you want?

Man

Zerkov and the others.

Girl

A tall man with a mustache?

Man (eagerly)

Yes, yes.

Girl (matter of factly)

They all left long ago.

Man

They can't have left. Don't lie.

Girl

You wanted to know, and I'm not lying.

Man

They have no right. They can't do this to me—they have no right!!

Girl

Why is it so important that you see them tonight—won't it wait until morning?

Man

No, it will not wait until morning. Mind your own business.

Girl

What did they do to you then? Are you sure you're feeling well? Why don't you sit down?

Man

Yes, yes, I will sit down—thank you.

(pause) When did you say they left?

Girl

At least two hours ago—it's after three now.

Man (urgently)

Did they say where they were going?

Girl

No.

Man (insultingly)

Have they paid you not to tell me? Well, I will pay you to tell me. Here, look, I have money. I had to borrow it—but, here it is. You mustn't think me as shabby as I appear. Once I—well, I was as grand as Zerkov—Now, then, where did they go?

Girl

I've already told you, I haven't the slightest idea. I would tell you for nothing if I knew—it's nothing to me.

Man

But they've warned you I was following them—eh? What did they say about me? Did they tell you I was after them? Did they tell you how they disgraced me, and that I wouldn't stand for it? Did they tell you, did they?

Girl (rather frightened)

They didn't say a word about you, so far as I know. You might ask the other girls—the ones they went upstairs with. But you'll have to wait until morning.

Man

Wake them up— I'll ask them now.

Girl

That's out of the question—the girls have earned their sleep. Some of them have gentlemen with them.

Man

I'll pay, I tell you.

Girl

Look, mister, you're really carrying on in a disgraceful way. This is a very respectable house— We never have any trouble with the police—and Madame won't put up with nonsense like this. Men who come here—patrons—are expected to behave like gentlemen. If you don't behave yourself, you'll have to leave.

Man

Ha, ha, ha!

Girl

What's so funny?

Man

To be lectured on manners by a little whore. Well, it's a fitting conclusion for this night.

Girl

You needn't have said that. It seems to me I've been very patient with you, and treated you as a gentleman. Now, if—

Man

Forgive me, forgive me. You have been more than patient, you have been kind. You are a saint, a Madonna. You rebuke me very justly.

(wildly)

Let me fall at your feet, sinner that I am.

(he kneels)

Bless me!!

Girl (furious)

Get out!! Get out!! Do you make fun of me, too? Get out!!

Man

I am not making fun of you. Madonna, bless me, for I have sinned; I am abject; I am worthless; I am not worth your little finger.

Girl

Do you enjoy mocking me? What have I done to you? Why do you come here to make me miserable?

Man

No, no. Don't misunderstand, I am sincere.

Girl (shaken)

Please, please, get up. Stop talking like that. You are delirious, you poor man. Here, sit on the couch.

Man (letting her lead him)

Thank you, thank you.

Girl

Would you like some brandy?

Man

I think so—yes. It might help.

Girl

It's two and a half roubles.

Man (fingering a large roll of bills)

Here, here.

Girl

This is almost fifty—it's much too much.

Man

I don't want it—keep it.

Girl

Really, you can't just throw your money away.

(She forces it back on him.)

You must be careful what you do, brother, or you won't have any money to your name.

Man

What does it matter?

Girl (giving him some brandy)

Are you feeling better?

Man

Yes, thank you.

Girl (quickly, but not really concerned)

Would you like to go upstairs with me?

Man

How much does that cost?

Girl

Fifty roubles. I'll give you a discount at this hour. You can have me and the brandy for fifty roubles, how's that?

Man (preoccupied with other thoughts)

Later, perhaps.

Girl

But, it's late already. What else is there to do? I won't go below forty-five, no matter what. I never sell myself short.

Man

Sit here, and talk to me.

Girl (cheerfully)

I'm much better at what I do upstairs than I am at talking, you know.

Man (rather desperate)

Please, I want to talk just now. It's extremely important to me to have contact with another human being.

Girl (yawning)

As you wish. But, I'm very tired, and I don't know what I should charge you for talking. You're keeping me awake. Maybe I should charge you extra for that, I can make love in my sleep.

Man

Why do you talk like that?

Girl

Like what? I was just making a joke.

Man

So cynically.

Girl

Was it cynical? Well, I suppose you're right.

Man

You're a nice girl.

Girl (faintly amused)

Am I? Then what am I doing in a place like this?

Man

That's what I wanted to know.

Girl

Well, you see, it all started when I was a little girl—my stepfather was always making eyes at me, and then one night—

(laughing)

How do you like that? Or, would you prefer the one that goes—I was a sweet little country girl and I fell in love with a soldier. And, you see, there was, well, a child, and my father, pious man, threw me out. Do you like that better?

Man

Can't you see that I'm being sincere?

Girl

Can't you see that I'm not?

Man

On the contrary, you strike me as being totally sincere.

Girl

I wish you hadn't said that.

Man

Why?

Girl

Because you understand me. I'm afraid I may tell you the truth—and that might be very—unpleasant. Why must you be so serious?

Man

I want to help you.

Girl

What makes you think I need help? I do quite well here.

Man

We all need help.

(A silence descends upon them. The Man goes to the window.)

Man

The weather is beastly.

(The girl does not respond to this remark.)

What's your name?

Girl

Lisa.

Man

Were you born in these parts?

Lisa

No.

Man

Where do you come from?

Lisa

Riga.

Man

Have you been here long?

Lisa

Been where long?

Man

In this house.

Lisa

A couple of months.

Man

Are your parents alive?

Lisa

Yes. I mean, no.

Man

Where are they?

Lisa

In Riga.

Man

And what do they do?

Lisa

Nothing.

Man

What do you mean, nothing?

Lisa

They're tradespeople.

Man

Have you always lived with them?

Lisa

Yes.

Man

Why did you leave them?

Lisa

Is that any business of yours? No reason.

(They are both silent, then the he tries a new approach.)

Man

I saw them carrying a coffin yesterday, and they nearly dropped it.

Lisa

A coffin?

Man

Yes, in the Haymarket. They were carrying it out of a cellar, you know, from the basement of a—a place like this.

Lisa

I don't understand.

Man

A whorehouse. It was filthy all around. Eggshells, litter, a stench. It was loathsome.

(Lisa makes no response.)

A nasty day to be buried.

Lisa

Why?

Man

The snow, the mud, the dampness.

Lisa

It makes no difference.

Man

No, it was horrid. There must have been water in the grave.

Lisa

Why should there be?

Man

Because the place was waterlogged. It's a regular marsh. I've seen it myself—many times.

Lisa

I still don't see what it matters. You're dead, you're dead. You don't care.

Man (increasingly nettled)

Do you meant to say you don't care how you die?

Lisa

Not much. But, why should I die?

Man

Well, someday, you must.

Lisa

I suppose so. But, why think about it?

Man

You will die just like that girl. She was young, like you. She died of consumption.

Lisa

So. You have to die of something. Anyway, we don't have Camilles in Russia. Here, she would have died in a hospital.

Man

You seem to think you know all about it. In the first place she was in debt to her Madame. She had to work right up to the end.

Lisa

You seem to know her so well. Were you a regular of hers?

Man

No!! I heard some soldiers talking. They were going to a tavern to drink her health.

Lisa

Well, she had that, anyway.

Man (irritated)

And, is it better if she died in a hospital?

Lisa

I don't see what difference it makes, really. One place is as good as another to me.

Man

We'll see, we'll see. Your time is not far off—

Lisa

What do you mean by that? Why should I die?

Man

If not now, then a little later.

Lisa

Why are you so morbid? Why a little later? Why not after a long time?

Man

Why? Now, you are young and fetch a high price—

(Lisa laughs)

But, in a year or so, you will be different— and then— Well, too bad—

Lisa

In a year?

(touching her hair)

I don't think it shall be as soon as that—

(laughing)

This life is not as hard as some people think it is—

Man

Anyway, in a year or so, you will be worth less. And then you will go into a cheaper house. Then to another—and keep going—until you wind up in a Haymarket basement. That is, if you're lucky, and don't catch some disease.

Lisa

Oh well, then I shall die.

Man

But one is—sorry.

Lisa

For whom?

Man

For life.

Lisa

I think you read too many sob stories.

(They are both silent, then the Man tries again.)

Man

Have you been engaged or married?

Lisa (flaring)

What's that to you?

Man

I'm not prying. It's nothing to me. Why are you so cross? Of course, you may have had your troubles. What is it to me? I simply felt sorry—

Lisa (mocking)

For life?

Man

For you.

Lisa

You needn't trouble yourself.

Man

I don't see any reason for you to be so rude. I've been very polite.

Lisa

Condescending.

Man

Do you really think you're on the right road?

Lisa

I never think anything.

Man

That's your trouble: you refuse to think. Realize, while there's still time. There still is time. You are young—good-looking. You might still love, be married, be happy.

Lisa

Being married won't necessarily make you happy.

Man

So, that's it. But it's much better than the life here.

Lisa

No. It's not.

Man

With love, you can live, even without happiness. Even in sorrow, life is sweet. But here!

What is there but filth?

Lisa (archly)

Then, what are you doing here?

Man

Never mind my being here. I was drunk when I came here.

Lisa

You still are.

Man

Maybe I'm worse than you are— But with a man it's different. Whatever I do, I'm nobody's slave. I shake it off in the morning and start all over again.

Lisa

And what makes you think I can't shake it

off?

Man

Because, a whore is a man's slave.

Lisa

But, many men are slaves to their whores.

Man (savagely)

A whore is every man's slave.

Lisa

Only if he has the price.

Man

And, do you have the price to get out of here? Admit it—you're in debt to your Madame.

(Lisa says nothing.)

Man

There, you see! And, don't think you'll ever get free of her. She'll see to that. But, don't misunderstand me, I'm not trying to annoy you.

(maudlin)

Perhaps I, too, am just as unfortunate— How do you know? With me, it's like drink.

(grabs her)

Tell me, is this loving? Is this how one human being should meet another?

(kissing her) It's hideous, isn't it?

Lisa (slowly)

Yes—it's hideous.

Man

So, so—you, too, are capable of certain refinements. I knew there was a point of likeness between us.

(holding her face in his hands)

Yes, you have an innocent look. And so young. It's difficult for you to understand what it means to a man like me to have someone who—

Lisa

Who—?

Man

It's hard to explain. Someone to talk to, to explain things to. To make her understand life. Yes, it's interesting

(pause—then with a note of authority)

Why did you come here?

Lisa

Oh, I don't know.

Man

But, wasn't it much nicer at home?

Lisa

It's really much nicer here in every way.

Man

So, that's it. You are not sentimental. If it were better at home, you surely would have stayed there. It's not likely a girl like you would come here of your own inclination.

Lisa (ironic)

A girl like me?

Man

So, you think I'm flattering you? Well, perhaps I am. Anyhow, I'm convinced someone has wronged you.

(Lisa is silent.)

You see, if you had a proper childhood, you shouldn't be so unfeeling. However bad it may be, a home is a home.

(Lisa is silent)

I grew up without a home.

(Her continued silence angers him; his maudlin appeal for sympathy has been rejected)

If I had a daughter, I believe I should love her more than my sons,—really.

Lisa

Why so?

Man

I almost thought you weren't listening. Well, to be honest, I don't know. But, I used to know a very hard man once who would practically go down on his knees to his daughter. He was mad about her. He would go about in rags, but he would spend his last penny on her.

Lisa

It would be nice to have such a father.

Man

Fathers always love their daughters more than mothers do. As for me, I don't think I'd ever let my daughter marry.

Lisa (laughing)

What next?

Man

I should be too jealous—really, I would. To think that she would kiss anyone else. To think she should love a stranger more than her father.

Lisa

You're funny.

Man

I amuse you, do I?

Lisa

You don't know anything of life.

Man

For example?

Lisa

Some fathers are happy enough to sell their daughters, rather than marry them.

Man

That's terrible. Such things happen only in families without either love or respect for God. Such families exist—but, I am not thinking of them.

Lisa

Have you come here for nothing else but to torture me?

Man

I am sorry—perhaps I am torturing myself.

Lisa

Now, let me ask some questions—why are you so insistent on finding your friends?

Man

Insistent—I?

Lisa

Yes, why were you so insistent?

Man

I refuse to be cross-examined by you!! If I was excited, it's only natural, after all, I'd been insulted— I have a natural right to show my indignation. It's none of your business.

Lisa

You didn't come here to engage my services. Surely, you didn't come here to hold my hand. Why did you come here?

Man

I came here—none of your business why I came here.

Lisa

Then, what makes it your business why I came here?

Man

I'm not trying to pry into your life. I saw you, and I took pity on you—that's all.

Lisa

How dare you come here and pity me?

Man

Well, what do you want? Do you want me to call you whore and throw stones at you? Is that what you want?

Lisa

Stop it. I just want you to mind your own business and respect my privacy.

Man

What has the world come to? Little whores are now insisting on their right to privacy? What will be next? Pretty soon they'll want to vote.

Lisa

Please don't call me whore. Please.

Man

Lisa, I'm sorry. I didn't mean it. What can I say to you? I came here for reasons of my own. Perhaps, I should mind my own business. But, I like you, and you looked as though you wanted help.

Lisa

I—

Man

Yes, you look as though your eyes are crying out for help. With your tongue, you may frighten help away—but your eyes—seem to scream for it. And, even if I am mistaken, you certainly need help anyway.

Lisa

Not from you. I've seen your kind before. You can't help anybody.

Man

Oh, Lisa, can't you see where this kind of life is leading you? You're still young and pretty. You can laugh now and enjoy it—but how will you feel in a few years?

Lisa

Let me ask you one thing— If I weren't young and pretty, would you care what happened to me at all?

Man

I honestly don't know, Lisa. But, my heart goes out to you. Perhaps, if you were old and ugly, it wouldn't. I should like to think it would—

Lisa

That's honest, anyway. I'm sorry if I'm being rude.

Man

You're shy and sensitive, aren't you? And you try to hide it under irony. Only it doesn't work too well, does it?

Lisa

Not with you.

Man

Perhaps there are compensations. Perhaps the

management allows you to have a lover to comfort you. Do they let you have a lover, Lisa? Do they?

(Lisa turns away)

But, what good is he, if he takes you back after other men have touched you? If he lets you go from his arms to other men—?

Lisa

I think the Devil must have sent you here.

Man

Do you think he will marry you? Why not ask him? Or, are you afraid to hear his answer?

(Lisa is increasingly uncomfortable)

Worthless, as he is, he would only laugh at you. And beat you, too, for asking. Does he beat you, Lisa?

Lisa

What must I do to make you stop? Have I done you any harm? Why won't you leave me alone?

Man

Lisa, please, I'm only trying to help you, to make you think about your situation.

Lisa

Don't you see, that the only reason my situation is bearable is that I manage not to think about it?

Man

Lisa. Lisa, that's just the point. As long as you deceive yourself, life will be bearable. That is precisely what I must prevent by making you think.

Lisa

Why don't you want me to be able to bear my life?

Man

Because it's bad for you; it's an evil life.

Lisa

It's worse to think about it. Nothing is bad, if you don't think about it.

Man

But, you can stop. Unless you realize where it is leading you, you'll continue down this road.

Lisa

But if there's no way back—?

Man

Lisa, there's always a way back. Take me, for example: I came here tonight in a drunken state because my friends insulted me. I wanted revenge. If only I could hold my liquor. I came here because they came here. I was proud—I wanted to create a scene. Then, I saw you, and a nobler thought came to my mind—

Lisa

You talk like—like a book.

Man

(furious, but controlling himself)

Perhaps my way of expressing myself is slightly academic. I am a writer and a student. Maybe I don't know how to use the language of the people—of everyday life. But I am sincere, Lisa. Certainly, if you had the least understanding of goodness and decency, you would appreciate what I have been trying to do. I have been trying to improve your mind with my culture. Oh, Lisa, if you would not harden your heart, what friends we could be. All sorts of things might happen.

Lisa

Like what?

Man

I can see I've been wasting my time on you. You're beneath my notice—beneath the notice of any decent man. You're beyond redemption. Go and wallow in the filth you love.

(He picks up his coat and jacket and makes a big fuss of getting ready to go, just like a parent threatening to leave a child to terrify it. His tactics have finally proven successful: Lisa is sobbing violently.)

Lisa

Don't go, please don't go. I have so much to say to you. I want to leave here. I need your help. I want it. I'm sorry for the dreadful things I said.

Man

Lisa, I'm sorry, don't cry. I didn't mean it, really, Lisa, I didn't mean to hurt you. I was wrong. Forgive me, my dear.

Lisa

You're so kind.

Man

But, I really must go now. Here.

(he scribbles his address)

This is my address. Come to see me.

Lisa

Oh, I will, I will.

Man

I've got to go now.

Lisa

Wait a minute.

(She rushes to a small desk and removes a letter.)

Here, you see.

(Lisa gives him the letter and he reads it.)

Man

It's a very lovely love letter. Who is he?

Lisa

He's a medical student in Riga. He knew me when I lived there. I met him a few weeks ago here. Of course, he has no idea what I'm doing now. Isn't it wonderful?

Man (listlessly)

Yes, it's very nice.

Lisa

But, what shall I do? Can I marry him, as he asks me to? I mean, would it be right, without telling him? And, how can I tell him? I'd rather die than have him know—and—and—well, that's all, I guess.

Man

I think you should postpone your decision until after you have left here.

Lisa

Yes—of course—you're entirely right—but—

Man

It's up to you, Lisa. I shall be waiting to help you. Now, I am going, Lisa.

(he puts on his hat and leaves)

Lisa

(paces up and down a bit after he leaves, clutching her letter)

But, what if I haven't the courage?

BLACKOUT

ACT II.

Scene 2

A garret apartment occupied by the Man of Act I. There is a door to the back, to the audience's left. The Man is talking to his servant, Apollon.

Man

Why can't you clean this place up? It would be horrible if a certain person that I'm expecting should see the way you force me to live.

Apollon

You've been expecting a certain person to come for the last two weeks—and you know very well this certain person is the last person you want to see.

Man

I order you to clean this place up; it's what I pay you for.

Apollon

Pay!! Ha.

(Apollon now simply stares at the Man. The latter becomes nervous.)

Man

Ah—so you're up to your old tricks of staring again. Stop looking at me like that. For ten roubles a month—a good wage—you consent to do absolutely nothing for me and scorn me in the bargain. For seven years you have tormented me and you simply will not go away. Well, I won't pay you your wages if you won't work, and you can stare at me all you like. You haven't earned them and you shan't have them, do you hear?

(Apollon continues to stare at the Man for a while and then walks out. The Man breathes a sigh of relief. Apollon reappears.)

Man

What do you want now?

Apollon

Nothing.

(He looks at the Man and sighs)

Man

I won't do it, I tell you, I won't pay you. Because—because I don't wish to, and I'm the master. If you were respectful—I might—but otherwise you can wait till Doomsday for all I care.

(There is a knock at the door.)

Man

Wait—see who that is. I must straighten up.

(Apollon shrugs and goes to the door. The Man races about frantically trying to put the room in order but only succeeds in making it more messed.)

(Zerkov and Trudolyubov enter.)

Man

It can't be.

Trudolyubov

We came to apologize for the other night. We are very sorry about the whole thing.

Zerkov

It was an oversight—a misunderstanding.

Man

Your apologies are a little late coming.

Zerkov

But, you see, it isn't our fault. We were going out of town—that's what the party was for. We were dreadfully sorry that you got the wrong address. It was all the fault of that stupid waiter. One should never have trusted things to him. He forgot entirely to tell you, and he forgot to tell us until it was too late to tell you we had changed the place of our meeting.

Man

I hunted all around for you. It had the appearance of a deliberate insult.

Trudolyubov

Can you think we would do such a thing to an old friend? That's uncharitable.

Zerkov (ironically)

Certainly we would not want to lose the favor of your wit. We could not be guilty of such baseness to one we value so highly.

Trudolyubov

Did you wait long?

Man

For almost three hours. Then I went around to your usual haunts and eventually found you had adjourned to Madame Sophie's. I went there, but when I got there, I found you had left.

Zerkov (sniggering)

So you scented us out. Bravo! But I hope you did not find your evening altogether wasted. There's a real nice little piece there named Lisa. Just your type, I should imagine.

Man

Never met her. If you mean to insult me further—

(They make signs of protest.)

It wasn't at all funny. It was—it was simply—absurd.

Trudolyubov

Absurd, and something else as well. It was rude. Unintentional, of course. And see, we didn't know your address, and there was no way to tell you there'd been a change in plans, so we had to leave a message with the waiter, and he, of course, forgot. Then we had to track you to this place. And so, here we are.

Zerkov

Tell me, what are you doing now?

Man

I work for the Naval Department.

Zerkov

Is it a good position? What made you leave your job with the Treasury?

(Zerkov speaks with a slight drawl)

Man (imitating the drawl)

I quit because—ah wanted to.

Zerkov

And the remuneration?

Man

What remuneration?

Zerkov

I mean your salary?

Man

Are you cross-examining me?

Zerkov (teasing)

Do you want a lawyer?

Man

Five hundred roubles a year, if you must know.

Zerkov

It must be hard to make ends meet.

Trudolyubov

Slave wages.

Zerkov

You've lost a lot of weight. You've really changed a lot.

Trudolyubov

Don't embarrass him.

Man

I'm not embarrassed. Let's talk of something more intelligent.

Zerkov

So you can show off your culture?

Trudolyubov

This is really stupid. Here we are, old friends

and classmates, squabbling like children.

Zerkov

He thinks he's better than I am, because he got better marks than I did when we were in school. Could anything be more ridiculous? I may have envied him his grades, but never as much as he envied me my money. Now for a display of wit.

Man

Sir, let me tell you, I hate phrasemongers and fops. That's the first point—and there's a second one to follow it. The second point is I hate smut and smutty talkers. The third point is I love justice, truth, and honesty. I love thought, sir. And I love friendship without condescension. Equality—that's it, I love equality. I should throw a bottle at your heads—but instead, I will simply tell you that I regard you as so many inanimate pawns.

Zerkov

I am very much obliged to you.

Trudolyubov

He wants a punch in the face for that. He's drunk.

Zerkov

So there you have it, ladies and gentlemen. We have seen a display of wit by a man of breeding. An intellectual of our times. An unsocial socialist.

(The Man starts to employ Apollon's tactics on them. He walks up and down without looking at them, whistling.)

Zerkov

There he is thinking if only we knew what a fine fellow he is, how we would hug him to us. Only the fact is, we do know. Come along, we've wasted enough time here.

Man (barring their way)

Don't go. I beg your pardon—I've insulted you. And you, too.

Trudolyubov

Ah, you don't care for dueling, is that it?

Man

I'm not trying to avoid a duel. I'm sorry, I want to be reconciled. I'll fight you, if you wish. You will fire first, and I will fire into the air.

Trudolyubov

He is comforting himself—

Zerkov

He's simply raving. But, let us pass. Why are

you barring our way?

Man

I ask for your friendship. I insulted you, but—

Zerkov

Insulted? You insulted me? Understand, sir, that you never, under any circumstances, could insult me.

Trudolyubov

That's enough for you. Out of the way.

(They brush him aside and go out. The Man stands momentarily in shock, and then screams for Apollon.)

Man

You brutes, you brutes. Either you will go down on your knees to me and beg me for my friendship, or I will slap you in the face. So, this is it, this is it at last—real life. Apollon!! Get me my coat— Hurry up, I've got to slap that man in the face.

Apollon

They will beat you.

Man

I will slap him, I say. Get me my coat. The blockheads will be forced to see the shame of it. We shall fight at day break—that's certain.

Apollon

But, where will you get pistols?

Man

I shall borrow them from—no, I'll ask for an advance on my salary to buy them.

Apollon

The boss won't give it to you.

Man

He must, I say, he must.

Apollon

And, where will you get a second?

Man

I'll ask my boss. He's bound to consent as a matter of chivalry.

Apollon

Ask a bureaucrat to be chivalrous? Don't be absurd.

Man

Then, I'll get the first person I meet in the

street.

Apollon

You're dreaming. What if they have you put in custody?

Man

In that case, I'll show them. When I get out, I'll—I'll pull his leg and bite him. I will tell everyone that he has driven me to this, because he refuses to fight.

Apollon

People will only laugh at you. You know that's right out of Pushkin.

Man (furious)

Do you want me to kill you, too? Oh, it's disgusting—disgusting. It's all the fault of that little bitch. If it hadn't been for her, none of this would have happened.

(perceiving that Apollon is staring at him)

Well, what are you staring at me for?

(Apollon shakes his head slowly)

You fiend, you torturer. You want your wages, but you are too proud to beg me for them. So you come here to worry me with your stupid stares. As if I haven't gone through enough. You don't have any idea how stupid you are—stupid, stupid—stupid!!

(Apollon turns away from him)

Listen, here's the money. See, look at it all. All there, but you're not going to have it. Not until you beg my pardon.

Apollon

That cannot be.

Man

It must be. I give you my word of honor, it must be.

Apollon

There's nothing for me to beg your pardon for. Besides, you called me a fiend and a torturer, for which I can have you arrested—it's insulting behavior.

Man

You are a torturer. Go, summon me. Go at once, and get a police officer.

(Apollon laughs at him)

Go on—or just imagine what will happen.

Apollon
Whoever heard of a man having himself arrested?

Man (shrieking)

Go!

(there is a knock at the door)

They've come back to apologize, I knew it. They've realized what a shame it is, what a tragedy. Go let them in. I will forgive them—

(Apollon admits Lisa.)

Apollon

Lady to see you.

Man

You!!

(collecting himself)

Won't you sit down?

(The girl, who is well-dressed, sits and looks

around her. The Man winces as he realizes she is aware of his poverty.)

Man

You have found me in a strange position, Lisa.

(speaking hurriedly)

No, no, don't imagine that I am ashamed of my poverty. No, in fact, I'm rather proud of it. I am poor, but honorable. It is possible to be poor, but honorable. Let me offer you some tea—

Lisa

No, thank you.

Man

Apollon, here are your wages. You see, I give them to you, but for that, you must come to my rescue. You must go down stairs, this instant, and buy some tea. You don't understand who this woman is. This means—everything.

Apollon

(pays no attention at first, then just as the Man is about to go to pieces completely, says)

Shall I get a whole portion?

(at a nod from the Man, he leaves)

Man

I'll kill him.

Lisa

What are you talking about?

Man

I will kill him, kill him. You don't know

what that torturer is to me. What he does—
He is my torturer, he—

Lisa

What's wrong?

Man

Give me some water—over there—

Lisa (fetching some water and giving it to him)

There—are you better?

Man

Yes. Lisa, do you despise me?

(Lisa does not know what to say and does not answer)

Lisa, why have you come here? Tell me—please.

Lisa

I—I want to get away from there altogether.

(a long silence)

Perhaps, I am disturbing you?

Man

Not at all. But, that's not the reason you came here. I'll tell you why you've come.

Lisa

I'd better go. I can see something's wrong.

Man

Oh no, you're not going to get away so easily. Why have you come? Answer! Answer! Then—I'll tell you. You've come because I talked sentimental slop to you. So now you're soft as butter and longing to hear it again. Well, I'm not in the mood. I was laughing at you then, and I'm laughing at you now.

(Lisa starts to cry)

Why are you crying? Yes, I was laughing at you. I had been insulted by the brutes who came there before me. I was going to challenge them, but they were gone. So, I vented my spleen on you. I had been humiliated, and I wanted to humiliate someone on my turn. You were the lucky person.

Lisa

I can't believe you are so cruel—so cynical.

Man

Yes, it is possible, my girl. I mean, do you really think I am a wandering missionary to the whores, come on purpose to save your dirty little soul? You really thought that? I only wanted to hear the sound of my own voice.

Lisa

But, you told me to come.

Man

Save you? Redeem you? From what? Power was what I wanted, then a little sport, to see the little whore squirm under my artfully delivered words. Why? Because I like playing with words. What I really want is for you to go to Hell. Do you have any idea how I cursed myself for giving you my address? It was a necessary part of the game that I give you an address. But, it didn't have to be a correct address. What a fool I was. The world can go to Hell, as long as I have my tea. What do I care whether you go to ruin or not? You have no idea how much I hate you for letting you see me like this.

Lisa

But, why should you hate me, why?

Man

Why? Because, I posed as such a noble savior to you. And now you see the real me. I said I'm not ashamed of my poverty. Well—the truth is that I am shamed of it—more than anything else in the world. And then, you walk in and find me squabbling with my servant just like an old peasant. And my servant jeers at me. Surely, you must realize I will never forgive you as long as I live for witnessing this. Yes, you must answer for it because I am a scoundrel—because I am the nastiest worm on earth and you have found me out. Others are no better, but they are never put to confusion the way I am. It's my doom to be insulted wherever I go. Well, why don't you go?

Lisa

How unhappy you are.

Man (sobbing)

People won't let me—I can't be decent. And now, you are the heroine, and I am a loathsome villain. Not pretty, is it?

Lisa (kindly)

Why won't you look at me? (he looks at her) Darling, can't you see it's all right, and that I love you?

Man

Yes, I understand your feelings. (He embraces her cruelly, and pulls her down to the bed in frantic lust. She is shocked at first, but then returns his embrace.) But, can you understand my feelings?

BLACKOUT

ACT II

Scene 3

(When the lights go up, Lisa is lying on the bed, crying. She is half clothed, and hasn't the energy to rise. The Man is pacing up and down.)

Man

I can't even say I'm sorry, Lisa, though I should be, for you're really a fine girl. You see, all you did was add a personal hatred to the senseless hatred I felt for you. Because, I know you are better than I am, I had to degrade you. In doing so, I've degraded myself even more. And so, you see, the only way your presence will be tolerable to me is when I'm degrading you—to get you back down to my level. It's not a one time thing, Lisa. You will always rise above me, afterwards. So, hadn't you better go?

(Lisa begins to dress)

Real life is terrible, you know. I love books and the peace they bring. Why should life be so cruel? Won't you please go away, Lisa? Can't you see there's no hope for either of us together. After all, the whorehouse isn't such a bad place. Contrary to what I said, I've known many a girl to lead a long and pleasant life in one. I was just prosing, you understand. And really, a woman who is as good in bed as you are—her future is assured.

Lisa (still sobbing)

Goodbye.

(She rushes out.)

Man

Here—wait. You forgot your wages. Well, well, we've finally got rid of her—now we can be at peace.

(Looks at the money and then covers his face. Suddenly, he rushes to the window and calls out.)

Lisa, Lisa, wait. I want you to forgive me. I want to apologize. I'll marry you— She's gone—didn't even look back. Gone forever.

(Enter Apollon. Apollon stares about the room and takes in what has happened. Then he stares reproachfully at the Man.)

Man

Well, back at last!! Well, stare away, you—you've got your work cut out for you this time!

CURTAIN

ABOUT FRANK J. MORLOCK

FRANK J. MORLOCK has written and translated many plays since retiring from the legal profession in 1992. His translations have also appeared on Project Gutenberg, the Alexandre Dumas Père web page, Literature in the Age of Napoléon, Infinite Artistries.com, and Munsey's (formerly Blackmask). In 2006 he received an award from the North American Jules Verne Society for his translations of Verne's plays. He lives and works in México.

www.ingramcontent.com/pod-product-compliance
Lightning Source LLC
Chambersburg PA
CBHW031654040426
42453CB00006B/306